Matheus Oliveira de Jesus

Practical Guide: Bodybuilding Training Periodization

Matheus Oliveira de Jesus

Practical Guide: Bodybuilding Training Periodization

Bodybuilding Training Periodization

ScienciaScripts

Imprint

Any brand names and product names mentioned in this book are subject to trademark, brand or patent protection and are trademarks or registered trademarks of their respective holders. The use of brand names, product names, common names, trade names, product descriptions etc. even without a particular marking in this work is in no way to be construed to mean that such names may be regarded as unrestricted in respect of trademark and brand protection legislation and could thus be used by anyone.

Cover image: www.ingimage.com

This book is a translation from the original published under ISBN 978-613-9-67348-3.

Publisher:
Sciencia Scripts
is a trademark of
Dodo Books Indian Ocean Ltd. and OmniScriptum S.R.L publishing group

120 High Road, East Finchley, London, N2 9ED, United Kingdom
Str. Armeneasca 28/1, office 1, Chisinau MD-2012, Republic of Moldova, Europe
Printed at: see last page
ISBN: 978-620-8-15941-2

SUMMARY

ACKNOWLEDGMENTS

First of all, I thank God for everything.

To my father Altair and my mother Ivanir, who are undoubtedly my greatest encouragers.

To my family who have always supported me.

To all my students, who have supported me in the most intense moments throughout my career.

To all my teachers at the Faculty of Physical Education of Santos.

To my friends at the Human Movement Epidemiology Laboratory, who always encourage me to keep studying.

PRESENTATION

This book covers the fundamental aspects of drawing up the periodization of a bodybuilding training program.

The aim is to offer a practical guide to the main topics related to bodybuilding.

The book is structured in four parts: In the first part, basic terms and concepts will be clarified, such as the physiological and biomechanical approach. The second part presents the principles of bodybuilding training and its main variables. The third part presents and discusses programs for different levels of training (beginner, intermediate and advanced). Finally, in the fourth part, the history of training periodization will be covered and the main concepts related to the subject will be duly explored. Also, how to control training loads.

Professor Matheus Oliveira de Jesus has sufficient practical and theoretical experience to structure this book, which is why he was chosen to create it.

CURRICULUM

Matheus Oliveira de Jesus

Master's student in Human Movement Sciences and Rehabilitation at UNIFESP - Campus Baixada Santista

Specialist in Exercise Physiology Applied to the Clinic at UNIFESP - Campus Baixada Santista

Graduated in Physical Education from FEFIS/UNIMES

Member of the Human Movement Epidemiology Laboratory - EPIMOV/UNIFESP

PART ONE - GETTING TO KNOW BODYBUILDING

1. Terms and definitions

Origin and definition of the word bodybuilding

Bodybuilding is a term that was coined in "Brazilian" Brazil to spread the practice of weight training in a commercial way. This terminology comes from the combination of the words "muscle and action". Despite this, the terminology used by researchers in the field is "resistance training" (Hopf and Moura, 2002). However, as the focus of this book is on a methodological approach that is practical and easy to understand, we will use the term bodybuilding.

It can be defined as the execution of localized biomechanical movements in defined muscle segments using external overload or the weight of one's own body (Guedes, 1997). It can also be used as a sport, such as Olympic lifting, and also as physical preparation for sports training in various disciplines.

Muscle strength

Force is a physics concept represented by the product of mass and acceleration (force = mass x acceleration). However, when it comes to performing movements and exercises, it is referred to as muscle strength. There are also different definitions in the literature, such as:

"The ability to exert muscular tension against a resistance, involving mechanical and physiological adaptations that determine strength in a particular movement" (Barbanti, 1979).

"It is the physical quality that allows a muscle, or a group of muscles, to produce tension and overcome resistance in the actions of pushing, pulling or lifting" (Tubino, 1984).

"The ability to exert muscular tension against a given resistance, overcoming, sustaining or yielding to it" (Guedes, 1997).

"It is the instantaneous measure of the interaction between two bodies. Force is characterized by its magnitude, direction and point of application". Or even "as the ability to overcome or react to external resistance through muscular effort" (Zatsiorsky, 1999).

"It is the maximum amount of force that a muscle or muscle group can generate in a specific movement pattern and at a given speed" (Fleck and Kraemer, 2007).

"Torque modulus exerted by a muscle or several muscles in a single maximum isometric contraction of unrestricted duration". In this case, the author suggests that it would not be appropriate to speak of dynamic, isokinetic or static strength. In the view of various authors, the above definition would be "maximum static force", which would certainly be the greatest manifestation of the strength of a muscle or muscle group for a given position (Enoka, 2000).

Therefore, regardless of how it is defined in the literature, muscle strength is a physical capacity, which is why it tends to develop with training. And by training it, we can get stronger as we overcome applied stimuli.

Muscle strength manifests itself in different ways, such as:

Pure (absolute) strength: this is the maximum capacity an individual has to overcome resistance, i.e. the maximum weight (load) they can lift in a specific body movement.

Endurance strength: the ability of the neuromuscular system to perform several repetitions of the same movement for a prolonged period of time.

Explosive strength: the ability of the neuromuscular system to produce force in a given unit of time (Prestes et al., 2010).

Muscle strength is produced by the action of skeletal muscles and there are 3 types:

Isokinetic: this is done through muscle action at a constant angular velocity. This makes it possible to measure the force in the rotational axis (known as muscle torque) over the entire range of movement (Terreri et al., 2001).

Static or isometric: uniform tension without total change and without sliding of the muscle fibers.

Dynamic or isotonic: increasing tension with changes in muscle fiber length.

Dynamic action is divided into concentric (positive), where the force produced is greater than the resistance offered (muscle shortening occurs), and eccentric (negative), where the tension generated, because it is lower, is exceeded by the load imposed (muscle lengthening occurs) (Guedes Jr, Souza Jr, and Rocha, 2008).

2. Physiology of weight training

The increase in muscle strength during training is basically made up of two types of adaptation: neural adaptation and an increase in muscle mass (Fleck and Kraemer, 2006).

Neural adaptations

Neural adaptation is a concept that can sometimes be misunderstood and ignored when designing training programs. When we start training, the first change that occurs is neural adaptation. The initial increase in muscle strength occurs more quickly than muscle hypertrophy, as it is related to neuromotor learning (Okano et al., 2008), i.e. significant changes occur in the morphology of the musculoskeletal system. (2003) cites an example with which it is possible to distinguish between the goal of weightlifters (maximum strength) and that of bodybuilders (hypertrophy). Figure 1 illustrates the adaptations resulting from weight training:

Figure 1: Types of adaptation to weight training.

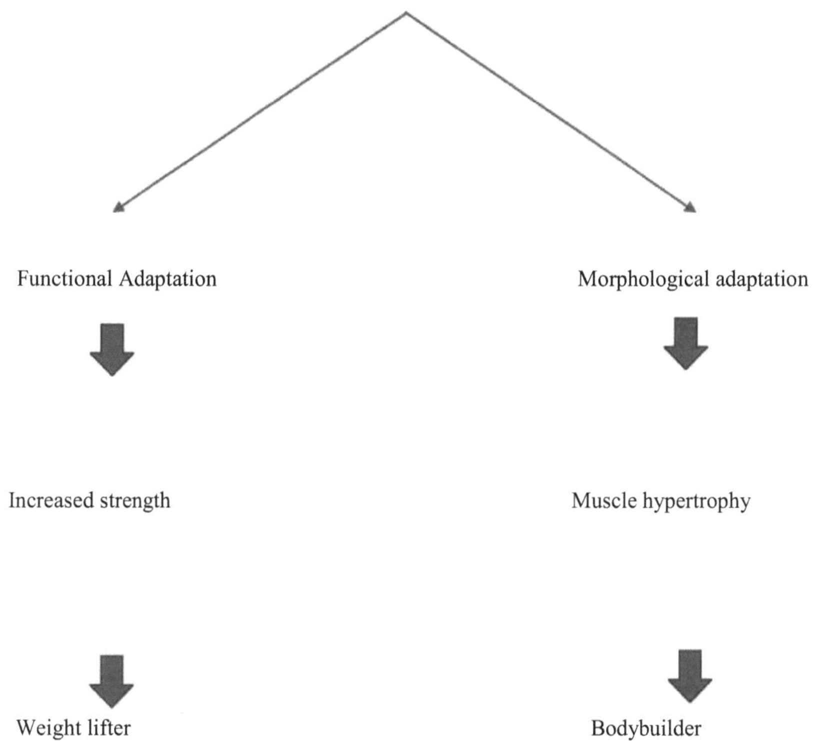

Figure 1.1: Weight training scheme.

Taken from Guedes Jr (2003)

To clarify figure 1.1, each athlete develops muscle strength through two adaptations. The weight lifter tends to develop maximum strength and, as a consequence, achieve hypertrophy. For the bodybuilder, muscle strength tends to increase by increasing muscle mass, and therefore increase maximum strength. In other words, for the former, training prioritizes neural adaptations, while for the latter, it emphasizes muscular adaptations.

According to the 2009 American College of Sports Medicine, strength gains in beginners are greater and faster than in more advanced students due to neural adaptation.

Rapid gains in strength due to neural adaptation are achieved by:

Intermuscular coordination

The first neuromuscular adaptation that occurs at the start of training is intermuscular coordination, which is the adjustment of the increased innervation of the muscles involved in a particular motor action. This can be explained by the improved coordination of agonist and antagonist muscle groups, which helps to increase the activation and recruitment of motor units (Teixeira and Guedes Jr., 2009). In other words, it allows for a more economical and synchronized movement.

Intramuscular coordination

The second adaptation resulting from the start of training is intramuscular coordination, which appears as one of the main adaptations at the start of training, and its function is to recruit motor units, related to the amount of information coming from the nervous system to the activated muscles and improving the reception of this information increases activation, and this is one of the first changes in the neuromuscular system (Bacurau and Navarro, 2001). To do this, we need to understand the theory of motor unit recruitment:

The theory of motor unit recruitment is based on the constitution of a motor neuron and all the muscle fibers it innervates. Motor units are classified according to the number of muscle fibers each motor neuron innervates. Muscles that perform high-precision movements, and large motor units, when a single neuron innervates hundreds of muscle fibers, such as muscles that perform low-precision movements (Billeter, 1992).

The increase in muscle strength is due to neural adaptations:

Number of motor units recruited:

When the intensity of the load to be overcome increases, the number of motor units to be recruited also increases. In addition, the recruitment of these motor units occurs more synchronously (Hakkinen, 1985). In this way, the greater number of muscle fibers capable of contracting at the same time provides a greater capacity for the muscle to produce force. It is worth remembering that not all motor units will be recruited voluntarily (Guedes Jr, 2003).

Size of the motor units recruited

The order in which motor units are recruited respects the so-called "size principle". This means that for lower intensity efforts, the smallest motor units are called upon first, i.e. a motoneuron that innervates a few muscle fibers. As the intensity of the load increases, the larger motor units are required, i.e. those that innervate hundreds of muscle fibers. The smallest motor units innervate slow twitch fibers, while the largest innervate fast twitch fibers (Basaldella et al., 2015). In explosive movements, where the speed is maximum but the force produced is well below the maximum isometric force, it is very likely that the law of size will not be respected and therefore the large motor units will be preferred and immediately recruited (Badillo and Gorostiaga, 2001).

Frequency of impulses in each motor unit

When an electrical impulse stimulates a particular motor unit, it may or may not be activated. However, a single impulse is not capable of producing muscle action (McArdle, 2011). Muscle action is therefore the sum of several electrical impulses per unit of time. And so, the frequency of impulses in a given motor unit is expressed in Hertz (Hz), which means the number of impulses that reach a motor unit in the space of 1 second. The higher the frequency (Hz), the greater the voltage produced.

Graph 1.1: Frequency of stimuli in a motor unit and production of tension during muscle contraction.

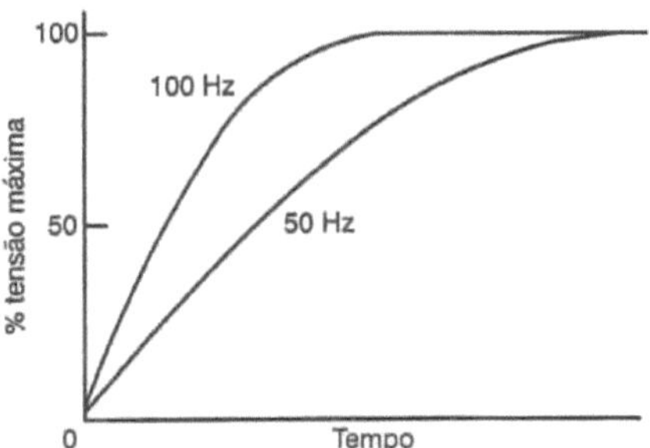

Taken from Guedes Jr (2003)

Inhibition of the OTG (Golgi Tendon Organ) and stimulation of the muscle spindle

As training progresses, the body tends to increase the sensitivity of the nervous system and this causes safety devices to become more activated. One of these is the Golgi Tendon Organ (GTO), which is a safety device to prevent excessive force being generated during a muscular action (Powers and Howley, 2005).

Training optimizes the action of the muscle spindle through the Stretch-Shorten Cycle, thus increasing the sensitivity of gamma motoneurons, which are capable of stimulating the recruitment of more motor units (ACSM, 2009). Reducing the inhibitory action resulting from the OTG tends to increase the production of muscle strength (Badillo and Gorostiaga, 2001).

Muscular adaptations

After a period of 8 to 12 weeks, strength gains peak through neural adaptations, while the increase in muscle mass becomes responsible for strength gains. This is due to adaptations such as hypertrophy, muscle fiber types, biomechanical and anatomical adaptations.

Hypertrophy

It is the continuous increase in the cross-section of muscle fibers (Guedes Jr., 1997) and is the main adaptation of the musculoskeletal system resulting from weight training. Factors such as age, gender, training frequency, nutrition, rest and genetics tend to influence gains.

Muscle hypertrophy can result from an increase in the concentration of ATP-CP, water and metabolites in the muscle cells, known as sarcoplasmic hypertrophy, and from the high level of tension imposed on the muscles, which we call myofibrillar hypertrophy.

Types of muscle fibers

Basically, muscles are made up of two main types of muscle fibers, classified as slow (type 1) and fast (type 2).

The classification of muscle fibers varies basically due to the predominant energy metabolism, the speed of muscle action and coloration (amount of hemoglobins). The table below illustrates the types of muscle fibers and their sub-classifications:

Table 1. Characteristics of muscle fiber types.

	Type I fibers	Type IIa fibers	Type IIb fibers
Metabolism	Oxidative	Glycolytic-oxidative	Anaerobic
Motor units	Slow with low excitability threshold	Intermediate with medium excitability threshold	Fast with a high excitability threshold
Fatigue resistance	High	Average	Low
Quantity of myoglobins	High	Average	Low
No. of mitochondria	Large	Medium	Small
Color	Red	Intermediate	White
Contraction speed	Slow	Intermediate	Fast
Type of exercise	Long duration/low intensity	Medium duration and intermediate intensity	Short duration and high intensity
Contraction force	Low power	Medium power	High power

3.   Biomechanical adaptations of bodybuilding practice

Through the muscular action of the muscles, various systems of body levers are formed in the musculoskeletal system. The purpose of these levers is to direct the production of force. Basically, a lever system has 3 basic components: the power of the muscles, the resistance in relation to gravity and the lever arms (bones). In addition, there are 3 types of body levers:

Interfixed: when the point of support is located between the resistance arm and the force.

Figura 2. Example of an interlocking lever.

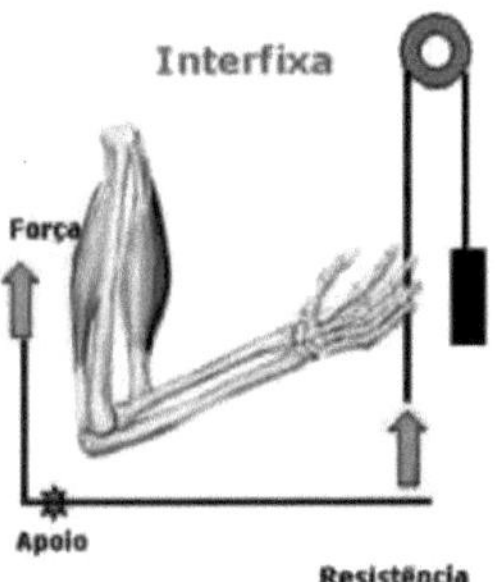

Interpotent: where the force is found between the point of support and the arm of resistance.

Figura 3. Example of an interpotent lever.

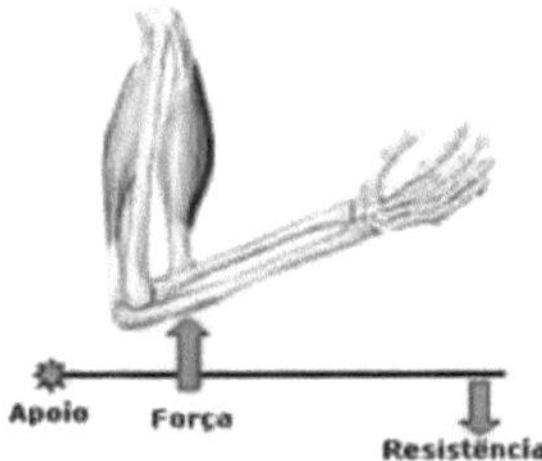

Inter-resistance: the resistance arm is between the point of support and the force, producing little speed.

Figura 4. Example of an inter-resistant lever.

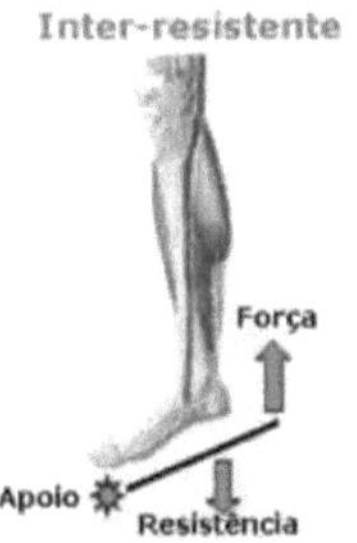

Although all types of body lever generate force, what we actually produce is muscle torque. Torque is a physical quantity associated with the possibility of rotation around an axis resulting from the application of a force to a body. This allows the functional classification of the musculoskeletal system into:

Agonist muscles: perform the main action of a movement.

Antagonist muscles: perform the opposite movement to the agonist, to regulate the speed of the movement.

Synergist muscles: perform the movement to try to stabilize a joint and prevent undesirable movements by the agonist.

Stabilizing muscles: they fix a segment of the body to allow basic support for the movements performed by other muscles.

Neutralizing muscles: have the function of neutralizing another muscle in which action is not desired in the movement to be performed (also called co-contraction).

PART TWO - METHODOLOGICAL ASPECTS OF MUSCULATION TRAINING

4.   Methodological aspects of bodybuilding training

By understanding the physiological effects and biomechanics of weight training, it is important to know what to take into account when prescribing training.

Methodologically, we must take into account the initial phase of training, number of sets, repetitions, speed of execution, interval between sets and exercises and the type of stimulus to be generated are fundamental to the practice of bodybuilding (Prestes et al., 2010).

In addition, it is important to know the biological and methodological principles of training in order to prescribe training, maximizing results and respecting the differences between individuals.

Principle of Biological Individuality

Each individual is characterized by a unique genotype (genetic characteristics acquired until birth) and phenotype (external characteristics from birth onwards) and therefore responds differently to stimuli (training). Therefore, the prescription of training must be individualized so that the results become efficient, quick and safe.

Based on this, the phenotype is capable of generating positive or negative changes in the genetic characteristics of individuals, which would directly result in the desired results. In short, it doesn't matter if an individual's genotype can lead them to become an Olympic champion in a sport if, throughout their life, they don't lead a regimented life of specific training, adequate nutrition and the necessary rest. And this could even change the genotype of their children and grandchildren.

In short, this principle should be understood as the need to individualize training programs so that not only functional and structural adaptations are more efficient, but also so that the process of adherence to physical exercise is more effective (Prestes et al., 2010).

Principle of Adaptation

The word adaptation is related to the act of adapting, reorganizing or restructuring oneself according to a new or unusual environmental situation.

Dr. Hans Selye, in 1936, created the Theory of the General Adaptation Syndrome, defining stress as a state in which a large part of the body deviates from its normal resting condition and, therefore, regardless of its origin, develops a syndrome that contributes to the body's adaptation. Depending on the intensity and frequency to which the body is exposed in stressful situations, the adaptation generated can be positive or negative.

The General Adaptation Syndrome (Selye, 1959) is divided into three stages:

1- **Alarm phase:** characterized by arousal.

2- **Resistance phase:** characterized by the physiological changes necessary to maintain the organism during the stress situation and afterwards. It depends on the duration and intensity of the stress, leading to positive adaptation.

3- **Exhaustion phase:** characterized by the body's inability to maintain the physiological changes of the previous phases, which causes it to succumb to stress, causing negative adaptations or plateaus. Adaptation, then, is nothing more than the adjustment that the body makes to its physiology in order to cope with stressful situations.

The relationship between stimulus and recovery is what we call the overcompensation cycle. All the alarm actions carried out by the body during an exercise session prepare it to maintain life under an unfavorable environmental situation, which leads to greater mobilization of the body's energy and structural reserves.

Overload Principle

The classic definition of this principle is that the gradual increase in overload progressively increases the body's functional efficiency, thus increasing its work capacity.

Currently, it is understood as the need to manipulate the total training load over time, gradually and according to the physiological and psychological characteristics of each individual.

This principle is fundamental in the training development process as it is linked to the manipulation of all the variables in bodybuilding. Therefore, the important thing is to identify the appropriate moments for increasing and reducing overload in a training program.

Principle of Interdependence: Volume x Intensity

Volume - Quantity - How much?

Intensity - Quantity - How much?

Training volume and intensity are inversely interdependent, i.e. as volume increases, intensity decreases and vice versa. In some sports it is difficult to determine this relationship. However, in bodybuilding, this relationship is easy to understand. The greater the amount of weight lifted, the lower the number of repetitions performed, and therefore the lower the training volume. Intensity, on the other hand, is more qualitative and can differ from person to person.

Principle of Continuity vs. Reversibility

Continued training helps to improve performance over time. Stopping training leads to a reversal of the adaptations that have taken place, which we call detraining. This usually happens much more quickly than training. In addition, continuity is fundamental to the motivational aspect. This principle is related to the principle of adaptation, since continuity over time is essential for the body's adaptations.

Maintenance Principle

The maintenance of physical fitness can be sustained for a certain period of time, even by reducing the duration and frequency of training, as long as the intensity is maintained.

Principle of Specificity

Training prescriptions must comply with the specific characteristics of the sport in question and the biological individuality of each individual. This specificity includes, among other things, the predominant metabolic pathway, the muscle groups and the predominant muscular work regime and the manifestation of strength. When this principle is not taken into account, the results are detrimental to performance.

Principle of Awareness

Individuals who are aware of why they are doing their job are motivated to do it and, as a result, the results will be better.

Awareness-Motivation-Better Results

5.   Bodybuilding training variables

Based on the concepts presented in the other chapters of the book, the time has come to discuss how training programs should be set up. In this context, the physical education professional has a fundamental role to play, because the simple fact of lifting weights, requiring higher levels of muscular work than those with which the muscles are already accustomed, can be a sufficient stimulus to generate positive adaptations in terms of increased strength. However, the lack of long-term planning leads to a plateau or even a decrease in results.

From this, we are faced with the need to plan training in order to obtain the best possible results. This planning should be done by manipulating all the training variables involved in a bodybuilding session (Balsamo and Simào, 2005).

The main variables in bodybuilding training are based on the load (weight lifted), the repetitions, the sets, the speed of execution, the interval between sets and exercises, the order of the exercises and the weekly frequency. Based on these variables, training methods are developed which determine the volume and intensity of training.

Exercises

For a better understanding of the various exercises that can be used in bodybuilding, we will use their classification in terms of: the number of joints involved, which can be uniarticular (for one joint) and multiarticular (for two or more joints); and the kinetic and kinematic chain of movement, which can be open and closed.

Uniarticular exercises: also called analytical by many authors, these are **exercises** in which only one joint participates. Good examples are shoulder lifts, elbow flexors/extensors and knee flexors/extensors, as they only require the movement of one joint.

Figures 5 and 6. Single-joint exercises.

Multi-joint exercises: also called basic or multi-segment exercises by many, these are exercises that require two or more joints to perform a given movement. Exercises such as bench presses, pull-ups and squats are good examples of multi-joint exercises, as two or more joints are mobilized (Faigenbaum et al., 2009).

Figures 7 and 8: Multi-joint exercises.

As there is simultaneous movement of two or more joints, the greater the number of muscle groups required to perform the movement. In the examples above, the main muscles responsible for executing the movement are mobilized. For example, in the bench press, horizontal shoulder adduction is performed (anterior deltoid and pectoralis major) and those responsible for elbow extension (triceps brachii and anconeus). In the squat exercise, during the concentric muscle action phase, plantar flexion, knee and hip extension movements occur. For this movement to occur, the triceps suralis (gastrocnemius and soleus), quadriceps and gluteus maximus muscles act dynamically. During the eccentric muscle action phase, dorsiflexion, hip and knee flexion movements occur. At this point, the hamstrings, quadriceps, gluteus maximus and triceps sural group are the muscles responsible. In addition, the joints of the spine also act isometrically, because the erector spinae and quadratus lumborum act isometrically to support the spine in an extension movement.

Multi-joint exercises are efficient for gaining strength and muscle hypertrophy and can become a positive strategy for meeting various objectives (Faigenbaum et al., 2009; Acsm, 2009). Due to the large number of muscle groups mobilized in an exercise, the following advantages can be observed:

- Increased total training volume.

- Higher concentration of testosterone levels.

- Greater calorie expenditure will be promoted, aiding weight loss.

- Less time will be needed to work all the main muscle groups, and this strategy is interesting for those who have time as a determining factor.

According to Fleck and Kraemer (2006), another favorable adaptation to multi-joint exercises comes from the fact that they have greater specificity of transfer than single-joint exercises, i.e. the motor gestures of multi-joint exercises are more similar to the majority of sporting and everyday gestures, allowing for better applicability of strength in activities of daily living.

These and other adaptations are considered the main exercises in a training session, but it is up to the professional to consider the characteristics of each type of exercise and individual needs in order to develop an appropriate training program.

In relation to the analysis of kinetic chains and kinematics of movement, the difference between open and closed chain movements lies in the freedom of the distal segment to move in space and not support the body (Moser et al., 2010). In open chains, muscle contraction acts by moving body segments with their extremities free in space, such as knee extension in the extension chair. In the closed chain, these same extremities are static, as in the case of the squat or leg press exercise, in which the feet are fixed to a surface.

Figure 9 and 10: Open and closed kinetic chain exercises.

Example of an open kinetic chain Example of a closed kinetic chain

It is important to note that the use of different exercises for the same muscle group can change the pattern of muscle fiber recruitment, stimulating different motor units, which is a positive adaptation for increasing strength and muscle hypertrophy.

Weight lifted

In bodybuilding exercises, load is defined as the resistance imposed on muscular work (Guedes Jr., 2003). This resistance is quantified by weight and, in Brazil, is measured in kilograms (kg).

There are two ways of calculating the load of a given exercise: The first is obtained using a given percentage of one repetition maximum (1 RM). A repetition maximum represents the maximum load that an individual can lift in the concentric phase of an exercise. Currently, some authors prefer to use the concept of maximum dynamic voluntary muscle action or the maximum dynamic load test instead of the 1 RM test (Rocha and Guedes Jr., 2013).

If 1 RM corresponds to 100 % of the exercise load, the load is set from a given percentage of this weight.

Another method of calculating the training load is called the maximum repetitions zone (MRs). In this method, the maximum number of repetitions (or a range of repetitions) that the individual should perform is stipulated and the load is determined through the execution of the exercise itself. For example, if a range of 8 to 10 repetitions is chosen and the individual is able to perform 12, the load should be increased slightly (between 2% and 10%) so that the next set or session the number of maximum repetitions falls within the desired range (Teixeira and Guedes Jr., 2009).

This method has been proposed because the same percentage of 1 RM can provide different stimuli in different muscle groups, i.e. the RM values determined by the percentage of 1 RM differ between muscle groups, making prediction impossible.

Weekly frequency

Weekly frequency is the number of training sessions the student will do per week and is influenced by different adaptations such as: training volume, intensity, exercise selection and order, conditioning level, the individual's recovery capacity and the number of muscle groups trained per session (ACSM, 2009). The American College of Sports Medicine recommends a frequency of 2 to 3 times a week for a bodybuilding program for previously untrained individuals (beginners), with 48-hour intervals between sessions. These programs aim to work all the main muscle groups during training sessions, providing good results, according to the position adopted by the American College of Sports Medicine.

However, as the level of conditioning increases and, consequently, the volume and/or intensity, a weekly frequency of 4 to 5 times is recommended. To do this, it is necessary to split up the training by muscle group, i.e. not all muscle groups are trained in one training session. In this type of split, each muscle group is usually trained 1 to 2 times a week.

Advanced weightlifters, bodybuilders and individuals with experience in strength training train as often as 6 times, and it is common to see each muscle group being trained 2 to 3 times a week, or even just once a week, with very high intensity.

An important adaptation that should be taken into account is that scientific evidence suggests that the same muscle group should not be trained on consecutive days (Fleck and Simâo, 2008), but at intervals of at least 48 hours.

It's also worth remembering that higher intensities require longer intervals. Advanced students can use longer intervals between training sessions for the same muscle group, which can vary from 72 hours to a week in length. These intervals are necessary to minimize the effects of late muscle soreness due to the high intensity of the training, since the peak of this soreness occurs, on average, 2 to 3 days after the training session, and can last for up to 10 days (Kraemer and Fleck, 2007).

Execution speed

The speed at which the exercises are performed will always depend on the training objectives.

With regard to increasing muscle mass, it has been believed for some time that the speed of execution of bodybuilding exercises for this purpose should be slow, especially in the eccentric phase.

In fact, the speed at which the eccentric phase is performed must be controlled, given that the muscles develop greater tension during this phase. According to Kraemer and Fleck (2009), when a person reaches their maximum level of concentric dynamic strength, they have only reached approximately

80% of their maximum eccentric strength.

Therefore, adjusting the loads for each movement phase would be the most ideal, i.e. increasing the load by approximately 20% in the eccentric phase. However, as in conventional bodybuilding training the loads are not changed from the concentric to the eccentric phase, the best strategy to adopt in order to maintain optimum muscle activation is to decrease the speed of execution in the eccentric phase.

Thus, based on this idea, some training methods were mistakenly created that valued the execution of exercises in an exaggeratedly slow manner.

Student profile

In addition to the methodological variables, we have to take into account the student and the environment (training site), as these have an influence on the training prescription. Therefore, questions such as "For whom? For what? Where? When?" should be asked when the student starts training.

Therefore, adaptations such as gender, age, the student's goals, time availability, equipment availability and possible physical limitations (detected in the medical examination and physical assessment) must be taken into account, in accordance with your student's goals and needs.

Age

Children, adolescents and the elderly should be monitored more carefully, as their physical capacities are limited. More intense methods are not suitable for these groups.

Children and adolescents usually get bored more easily when they are subjected to constant training routines, as well as being naturally curious about trying out different exercises and training methods. For this audience, it may be better to change certain aspects of the training every week or two weeks, to avoid demotivation and consequently abandonment of the proposed program.

The intensity is not necessarily changed, but rather the variability of the exercises and methods applied. In addition to this psychological adaptation, it should also be considered that the constant change of exercises changes the angle at which the effort affects the joints and muscles, avoiding possible injury due to the saturation of the load at a given point.

Older people, usually from the age of 50 onwards, who have a more patient profile, psychologically don't need as much variation due to motivational aspects, although the argument of avoiding injuries due to overload at a specific point in the musculature for too long is also valid, as it doesn't depend on age. For this age group, very high overloads and extreme angles of movement should be avoided (greater angles can be experienced with very low overloads).

The age group between adolescents and the elderly, if they are healthy, is where high-intensity training is most recommended and where there are fewer restrictions, but of course, always respecting possible circumstantial limitations.

Sex

An important aspect to consider is that women tend not to be able to endure long periods of training due to psychological and physiological adaptations that can lead to demotivation compared to men. Therefore, individualized planning is of the utmost importance to maximize results. For these women, within the same planned intensity, it may be more convenient to vary the training methodology used a little more, or when this is not recommended or possible, then the exercises to be performed within this same methodology should be varied.

Objectives

The most important aspect of training, the goal, varies from person to person and so the method used must be chosen carefully. The most common goals are to increase muscle mass (hypertrophy), lose weight or improve quality of life.

To this end, the choice of training methods must also be linked to the student's age, level of conditioning and desired goal. And the adjustment of the plan must be used carefully, taking into account the physical capacity to be worked on, the rest time and the weekly frequency. For example, the rest pause and forced repetition methods tend to be used for muscle hypertrophy, while the circuit training method tends to be used for weight loss.

Availability of time

The length of the workout (time) varies according to the teacher's prescription, as you can use a shorter and less intense workout or a longer and more intense one. However, reducing the time and increasing the intensity for those who don't have much time can be a strategy for optimizing the student's time. Some methods that are applied at high intensity will be carried out in considerably less time than others that are not as intense. The choice of training methodology must take into account not only the student's goals, but also the amount of time the individual will have to dedicate to bodybuilding, i.e. the daily time of each session and the weekly frequency.

Availability of equipment

Another important adaptation for setting up training sessions is the logistics of the space you are working in. Some methods, such as the Circuit, the Combined Series and the Giant Series, require certain machines to be available to the practitioner at any given time. Usually the biggest limitation is not so much the lack of machines and other equipment, but their availability when the student is going to use them, since at peak times in gyms it won't be possible to have the necessary equipment in time, due to the large flow of people requesting the equipment.

Therefore, the time at which the athlete trains and the amount of machines and equipment available are also limiting factors in choosing certain training methods.

Physical limitations

Through a good physical examination by a competent doctor and the anamnesis, anthropometric examination, postural examination and others carried out by the physical educator, a detailed report on the student's physical condition and health is obtained.

Osteoarticular injuries, heart disease and postural deviations must be analyzed and taken into account when prescribing training, so that the methods and exercises chosen do not accentuate or even minimize these problems.

In addition to the adaptations considered above, it is also interesting to analyze, when training intensifies, the practitioner's morphological profile known as somatotype: the degree of mesomorphy, ectomorphy and endomorphy of each student (these nomenclatures discriminate between individuals in terms of their body composition). This can also be a parameter for the number of sets, repetitions and exercises to be prescribed (Pontes and Figueiredo Filho, 2010).

Mesomorphy: is the biotype that lies between ectomorph and endomorph. This biotype makes it easier to gain muscle mass in terms of volume, strength and tone.

Ectomorphy: is the biotype characterized by a slender body, with little muscle mass, but with muscle tone.

Endomorphy: this is the biotype with the lowest rate of metabolism, which leads to a greater amount of body fat. As a result, it is more difficult to achieve muscle tone.

Figure 11. Morphological profiles.

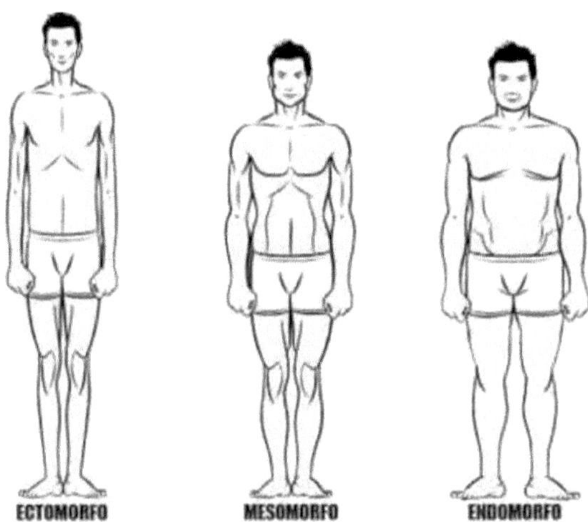

As training progresses and becomes more intense and sophisticated, biological individuality becomes increasingly important, and this is the main reference point for the physical educator to know which type of training will best meet the objectives of each student. It is because of biological individuality that there is no such thing as a cake recipe, a predetermined training prescription: each person responds differently to certain stimuli. In order to know which workout will work best for each person, certain parameters are used, such as anamnesis, physical assessment and personal experience in prescribing training.

At this point, the experience and training of the physical education professional is fundamental to achieving the desired goals more quickly and safely.

PART THREE: SETTING UP BODYBUILDING PROGRAMS

6. Training for beginners

The first phase of bodybuilding training is adaptation. At this first moment, the teacher gets to know the student and asks all the questions already mentioned in order to set up/prescribe the training, in which the student's specificity is not so important. Training is done at a low intensity and for a short period of time as it is an adaptive phase. Exceptions are made for special cases, such as orthopaedic problems.

So, regardless of the person and their possible physical limitations, most of the adaptation training is similar, as the low intensity won't entail any major risks that could compromise any of the systems involved in the process.

The main focus of adaptation to weight training is to improve motor coordination by learning the correct motor gesture and also to prepare the muscles, tendons, ligaments, joints and bone tissue for training, which will progressively become more and more intense.

This configuration seems to be the safest and most suitable for the vast majority of adapting individuals.

This methodology is aimed at beginners, i.e. students who have never practiced weight training or who have been idle for a long time. It is also an approach used for students of other disciplines who are just starting to train with weights.

To make the subject easier to understand, let's use two examples below: In the first situation we have a student who has never trained bodybuilding, in which case it would be more interesting to start with 1 to 2 sets per exercise, between 12 and 15 repetitions at low intensity. In the second situation, we have an athlete who is starting to train again, in which case it would be interesting to prescribe 2 to 3 sets, 12 to 15 repetitions, with moderate intensity, depending on the nature of the sport they practice (intensity and frequency of training, as well as the muscle groups involved in the sport). For example, soccer players tend to endure more sets and more intensity in the lower limbs than tennis players or swimmers.

In the initial phase of training, the sum of the sets performed is more than enough to promote the necessary adaptations and lead to changes in the systems involved, such as improved muscle coordination, overcompensation of muscle-hepatic glycogen and a small degree of muscle hypertrophy and bone mineral density.

Another important aspect to take into account is that the student doesn't have too much late muscle soreness, in order to proceed optimally with the adaptation. However, it is essential that the inflammatory process occurs in the muscle myofibrils, as this is an indicator that the breakdown of homeostasis is taking place. The overload, however, must be very well dosed, as it doesn't bring any benefits if it's too high; for sedentary people, any overload that produces a little resistance at the end of the repetitions already serves to produce the necessary adaptations.

Although it is still a very controversial subject, stretching exercises should be avoided in this phase, neither before, during nor after weight training, unless the individual already practices them (Garber et al., 2011). The tension produced in the muscles by this type of exercise will be added to the effort produced by the muscle-building exercises (stretching can contribute to the tearing of myofibrils), and will contribute to the appearance of late muscle pain when the individual exaggerates the time and intensity of stretching.

Despite the popular wisdom that "we should stretch to avoid muscle pain", stretching is absolutely not recommended in the first few weeks of weight training (Garber et al., 2011). Bodybuilding exercises alone provide positive responses in improving flexibility, when done correctly.

Warming up can be done in two ways:

Low-intensity aerobic activities: a walk on the treadmill with the aim of preparing the musculoskeletal structures by increasing body temperature, increasing blood flow to the recruited muscles, increasing neural activation and decreasing muscle stiffness (Simic et al., 2013). The speed at which the exercises are performed must be controlled so that there is no exaggeration which could cause the student late muscle pain.

Joint warm-up: warming up by performing the exercises that will be part of the training session with less intensity in order to prepare the joints involved during training. This process brings greater blood supply to the joints being trained and increases body temperature, generating better mechanical efficiency in muscle contraction.

As for the rest interval between sets, considering that the overload in adaptation is low, but you are still susceptible to muscle soreness, it takes 1 to 2 minutes to perform another set (Faigenbaum et al., 2009). Despite this, what really matters is the student's perception.

Example 1: General outline of the adaptation phase:

1 or 2 exercises per muscle group
8 to 10 exercises per session
1 to 3 sets of each exercise
12 to 15 repetitions in each set

Example 2: Training for beginners who train 3 times a week:

Exercise	Series	Repetitions
Bench Press	1 a 3	12 a 15
Bodyweight squat	1 a 3	12 a 15
Supinated handle	1 a 3	12 a 15
Leg press	1 a 3	12 a 15
Machine development	1 a 3	12 a 15
Extension chair	1 a 3	12 a 15
Seated rowing	1 a 3	12 a 15
Standing calf	1 a 3	12 a 15
Abdominal	1 a 3	12 a 15

Example 3: Weekly training schedule

Monday	Tuesday	Wednesday	Thursday	Friday	Saturday	Sunday
Training	Time off	Training	Time off	Training	Time off	Time off

Or

Monday	Tuesday	Wednesday	Thursday	Friday	Saturday	Sunday
Time off	Training	Time off	Training	Time off	Training	Time off

Didactically, the indication of only one set per exercise is best used when prescribing for the elderly, adolescents and people who have never trained bodybuilding. In this case, it is advisable to train this series 2-3 times a week on alternate days. You can also train the upper limbs and lower limbs alternately, or just the lower limbs first and then the upper limbs, or both upper and lower limbs.

An important point is that exercises other than those mentioned in the example can and should be prescribed, however, exercises with a large joint range and exercises with more precise and complex execution should be prescribed according to the observation of each student's motor coordination.

In short, the most important thing is to activate all the main muscle groups in the body, with just one exercise for each large muscle group in the trunk, the main muscles in the arms (biceps and triceps), shoulders and calves, and 2 to 3 exercises for the thighs (8 to 10 exercises per training session). In some cases, when the individual is very sedentary, you can choose not to activate the shoulders directly.

In this way, each muscle/group is worked 3 times a week, at a very low intensity, both in terms of the workload, which must necessarily be light, and the volume of sets per exercise.

If you prescribe 2 or 3 sets of each exercise, you can split up the workout to allow the muscles to recover better. For people who are able to train 4 times a week, you can divide the training into A and B (2 times a week training A, and 2 times a week training B). For people who only have 3 days a week to train, you can split training A, B and MIXED. Once a week training A, once a week training B, and once a week training MIXED, which repeats the main exercises from training A and B, ensuring that each muscle group is activated at least twice a week. Here are some examples:

Example 4: Division of the sessions by posterior and anterior part of the body.

Monday	Wednesday	Friday
Bench press	Seated rowing	Bench press
Leg Press	Vertical flexor	Leg Press
Oblique abdominals	Lumbar lying down	Seated rowing
Machine development	Direct thread	Vertical flexor
Adductor chair	Abductor chair	Machine development
Peck deck	Open handle	Adductor chair
Straight abdominal	Standing twins	Lumbar lying down
Triceps pulley	Lumbar lying down	Oblique Abdominal

Training should always start with exercises that work the larger muscle groups, such as the chest, back and thighs before the biceps, triceps and shoulders, calves and glutes. In this way, the energy potential that is greater at the start of the workout is directed towards the larger muscles that rely on agonists to execute the movement.

Example 5: Divide training into upper limbs and trunk, lower limbs and mixed.

Monday Training A Trunk/upper limbs	Wednesday Training B Lower limbs	Friday Training C Mixed
Inclined bench press	Squat with body weight	
Open handle	Leg press	Inclined bench press
Development with dumbbells	Adductor chair	Squat with body weight
		Open handle

French triceps	Abductor chair	Leg press
Alternating thread	Extension chair	Development with dumbbells
Oblique Abdominal	Flex table	Abductor chair
Complete Abdominal	Standing twins	Lumbar flexor table
Plank	Lumbar flexor table	Complete Abdominal

Example 6: Weekly split for beginners who train 4 times a week - Workouts A and B.

Monday	Tuesday	Wednesday	Thursday	Friday
Inclined bench press	Bodyweight squat	Rest	Inclined bench press	Bodyweight squat
Open handle	Leg press	Rest	Open handle	Leg press
Machine development	Adductor chair	Rest	Machine development	Adductor chair
French triceps	Abductor chair	Rest	French triceps	Abductor chair
Direct thread	Extension chair	Rest	Direct thread	Extension chair
Lumbar lying down	Flex table	Rest	Lumbar lying down	Flex table
Infra abdominal	Calf machine	Rest	Infra abdominal	Calf machine

As the increase in strength happens quickly at first, in 2 or 3 weeks of training, you can increase one more set for those who only did one set per exercise (100% increase in training volume), and one more set for those who did 2 sets per exercise (50% increase in training volume). In other words, regardless of how many sets you did, you could increase by one after 2 or 3 weeks of training.

Between the 4th[a] and 6th[a] week of training, the student should have improved their motor coordination for exercises that require a greater degree of balance and movement control, and also their skeletal muscles in processing the lactate produced during the exercises (although still in small quantities). Their intramuscular coordination should already allow for better recruitment of the related motor units, and possibly a little muscle hypertrophy can already be noticed.

It's important to remember that some people will adapt more quickly than others, since the adaptations described above will be influenced by biological individuality and external adaptations too. Students with higher testosterone levels, greater sporting experience prior to weight training and therefore better motor coordination, muscle fibers more suited to the training applied, adequate nutritional levels and correct sleep and recovery time, may have certain stages of adaptation shortened or even suppressed.

In the same way, some people will find it more difficult to master the correct technique for performing the exercises and more difficult to assimilate the training (recovery), with the occurrence of muscle and/or joint pain and fatigue beyond what is expected. These people will certainly have to spend more time in the adaptation period and intermediate phases before being exposed to advanced training methods.

7. Training for intermediate students

This phase starts between $4^a/6^a$ and 8^a weeks of training, just after the adaptation phase. In most cases, 4 weeks of adaptation is enough to increase the intensity and volume of training. At this point, we start to separate the muscle groups and isolate them on different days. In addition, we can also add advanced methods, although constant sets can generate the necessary adaptations to increase muscle mass,

With this division of muscle groups, bodybuilding sessions are divided into A-B-C, each workout is completely different from the other in terms of the muscles trained, requiring a weekly frequency of at least 4 days, ideally 5 days. As for the repetition count, you can stick to a range of 3 sets of 8 to 12 repetitions. The aspect that should be taken into account in this transition period of training is the increase in intensity where the practitioner should be encouraged to increase the overload of the exercises so that they feel difficulty in the last repetitions, from the first set of each exercise. In other words, they should feel greater resistance in all the exercises, compared to the training they did in previous weeks.

In training divided into three parts, certain adaptations must be observed. In addition to biological individuality, the principles of variability and overload are more important than the adaptation phase. Variability refers to the periodic change of exercises (and, with time, of methodology), so that the body doesn't get used to the adapted exercises. Priority, as has already been said, refers to the concept of training the muscles that need the most development first (when the body's energy is greater for those muscles), or training the larger muscles/muscle groups before the smaller ones.

Generally speaking, however, it is more usual to train the larger muscles before the smaller ones (chest, back and thighs before biceps, triceps, shoulders and calves). This is because if the smaller muscles are trained before the larger ones, they will be fatigued when they are required as accessory muscles, to the point where they will no longer be able to help the larger muscles train with the appropriate intensity.

To give another example, when training the back, in the vast majority of exercises we use the elbow flexors as the main accessory muscle, so if we train the elbow flexors before the back, they will be fatigued when they are required for back training (if these two muscle groups are trained on the same day), making the overload for the back smaller. As a result, the smaller muscles are trained with more emphasis than the larger ones, sacrificing the harmony of symmetrical development, as less intensity is directed where it is most needed.

Example 7: A-B-C training split.

Monday	Training A	Chest/Triceps/Shoulder
Tuesday	Training B	Back/Biceps/Trunk
Wednesday	Training C*	Thighs/glutes/calfs
Thursday	Training A	Chest/Triceps/Shoulder
Friday	Training B	Back/Biceps/Trunk
Saturday	Rest	
Sunday	Rest	

Start the following week with workout C, and the next with workout B.

Workout A: Chest/Triceps/Shoulder.

Exercise	Series	Repetitions
Bench press	3	8 a 12
Flying	3	8 a 12
Inclined crucifix	3	8 a 12
Peck deck	3	8 a 12
Triceps pulley	3	8 a 12
Triceps with rope	3	8 a 12
French triceps	3	8 a 12
Machine development	3	8 a 12
Lateral raise	3	8 a 12

<u>**Workout B: Back/Biceps/Trunk.**</u>

Exercise	Series	Repetitions

Open handle	3	8 a 12
Seated rowing	3	8 a 12
Unilateral rowing	3	8 a 12
Direct thread with bar	3	8 a 12
Alternating thread	3	8 a 12
Scott thread	3	8 a 12
Complete abdominal	3	8 a 12
Hip lift	3	8 a 12

Workout C: Thighs/glutes/calfs.

Exercise	Series	Repetitions
Leg press	3	8 a 12
Squat with dumbbells	3	8 a 12
Extension chair	3	8 a 12
Flex chair	3	8 a 12
Abductor chair	3	8 a 12
Adductor chair	3	8 a 12
Gluteus muscles	3	8 a 12
Glutes 4 supports	3	8 a 12
Standing calves	3	8 a 12

This division of training sessions into A-B-C, following 3 sets of 8-12 repetitions, can be followed for approximately 8 to 12 weeks, and possibly even longer, depending on the number of times you train and also on your goals and, of course, motivational aspect.

Within this period, (where logically the work characteristics have been increased in relation to training A and B), you can follow the same methodology, but periodically changing the exercises, to avoid too prolonged adaptations to the same angle of movement.

The exchange of exercises can usually take between 4 and 6 weeks, depending on the student's attendance, the logistics of the work environment and the student's goals.

It is also suggested to change the exercises of the training divided into A-B-C to avoid a plateau of stimulation on the trained muscles and also to increase the motivation of the practitioner.

Again, it's worth pointing out that this series divided into 3 can be maintained for a very variable period of time, or even always like this, depending on the training days available and the intensity. Normally, training is only divided into 4 (A-B-C-D) when the student has at least 4 days a week available to train, and when they have reached an optimum level of intensity in their training and muscle development.

8. Training for advanced students

After a few months of training, some students, especially those interested in higher levels of performance and better body composition, feel the need to increase their training. This happens both because the traditional sets don't have the same effect as they did months ago, and because of the monotony and psychological stress of always training in the same way, which causes demotivation in the medium and long term (Vieira, 2012).

Then, after the initial adaptation phase, and the subsequent A-B-C training phases, the practitioner will need more intense workouts, adding more advanced training methods, where you get away from the conventional way of performing sets and repetitions, such as the traditional 3 sets of 8-12 repetitions format.

In these cases, the workout can be divided into 4 or even 5 parts (A-B-C-D or A-B-C- D-E). This procedure is aimed at students who have acquired training experience, good muscle development and a reasonable physiological background, and who have at least 4 days a week to train. The main purpose is to intensify training in such a way that the trained muscle groups achieve better hypertrophy responses.

Another important factor is that with gradually increasing training loads, the total recovery time can increase substantially. For example, bodybuilders tend to perform sets for the same muscle group once a week due to the high volume and intensity of the training, although this type of training generates a lot of discussion.

To break homeostasis even further, if necessary, in addition to modifying exercises, sets and repetitions, is to modify the methodology, i.e. the way of training, radically changing some concepts.

In addition, we have to consider that we have a physiological limit for strength gains. After years of training, you can reach a plateau that is difficult to break. This happens from recreational students to bodybuilders and powerlifting competitors, who experience long periods of plateau in strength gains and hypertrophy. As periodically adding load to exercises is necessary for gains in hypertrophy and motor performance, if it is impossible to increase the weights used in training even more, we have the alternative of adding a different methodology, so that the correct stimulus is applied in order to continue making gains.

With this, your student won't just be dependent on increasing the weight of the exercises to increase muscle mass and/or achieve other goals.

Example 8: Weekly breakdown of A-B-C-D training.

Monday	Training A	Back/Biceps
Tuesday	Training B*	Thighs
Wednesday	Training C	Chest/Triceps
Thursday	Training D	Shoulders/Glutes/Calfs
Friday	Training A	Back/Biceps
Saturday	Rest	
Sunday	Rest	

* Start the following week with training B, and the next with training C.

Example 9: Weekly breakdown of A-B-C-D-E training.

	Monday	Tuesday	Wednesday	Thursday	Friday	Saturday	Sunday
Week 1	A	B	C	D	E	Rest	Rest
Week 2	A	B	C	D	E	Rest	Rest
Week 3	A	B	C	D	E	Rest	Rest
Week 4	A	B	C	D	E	Rest	Rest

Example 10: Weekly breakdown of A-B-C-D-E training.

Monday	Training A	Chest/Abdominals
Tuesday	Training B	Back/Biceps
Wednesday	Training C	Thighs-Glutes
Thursday	Training D	Biceps/Triceps
Friday	Training A	Shoulder/calf

| Saturday | Rest | |
| Sunday | Rest | |

In this example, you train every day from Monday to Friday without a break, leaving Saturday and Sunday for total rest. In this division, you get a good rest from one day to the next, because when you analyze the muscle groups trained, Monday's training has nothing to interfere with Tuesday's training, the same happening from Tuesday to Wednesday, on Wednesday you train your back, which doesn't interfere in any significant way when the athlete goes to train shoulders and triceps on Thursday, which in turn has no influence on Friday's training.

If the division is set up differently, (or even in this example), you can still train every other day, as the student may feel the need for more recovery between workouts, which will also depend on their lifestyle. The following division is suitable for students who train with very high loads (high intensity).

Considerations on the time interval between sets: this is a fundamental adaptation in bodybuilding training, as it regulates, along with the amount of overload used and the intensity of the training. Long and short intervals determine, respectively, lower and higher training intensity.

Very short intervals: these are intervals shorter than 30 seconds, allowing only partial recovery of the ATP-CP used during exercise in high-intensity workouts. If any lactate is produced during these sets, its dissipation from the muscles and blood is also compromised. Short intervals are generally used in circuit training.

Short intervals: longer than 40 seconds and shorter than 1 minute, have a wide variety of applications, used both in adaptation training (where the overload is low and requires less recovery time) and in traditional muscle hypertrophy training, around 1 minute of rest.

Medium intervals: intervals longer than 1 minute and up to 3 minutes, sometimes used in advanced muscle hypertrophy and strength training, as the overloads used require more recovery time to perform the next set with the same load as the previous set (recovery of the energy substrates used, metabolization of the lactate produced).

Long intervals: intervals longer than 2 minutes are necessary in maximal strength training, in which the overloads used are very high, necessary to recover the ATP-CP system used in the series that was performed, so that these loads can be used again in the next series.

This interval allows the student to satisfactorily resynthesize the ATP-CP system and also the cardiovascular system. Maximum strength training tends to produce very low amounts of lactate during its execution (alaerobic anaerobic training), so the long interval is only justified in terms of the ATP resynthesis aspect. Some lactate may be produced during the recovery phase of the sets, but this is not significant enough to negatively influence the training.

In short, respecting the rest interval is fundamental to successful training, and planning it correctly is just as important as choosing the number of sets, repetitions, type of exercise and weekly split.

Considerations on the range of repetitions: the range of repetitions to be used is still a matter of controversy and discussion among students and professionals in the field, as each student will respond differently to a given count. There is no scientifically exact number, no fixed count, as to how many repetitions would reproduce this or that effect on the musculoskeletal system. What does exist is a guideline regarding the repetitions indicated for each objective (ACSM, 2009).

Smaller repetitions with a higher overload are known as tension stimuli, and theoretically induce predominantly structural (myofibrillar) hypertrophy, i.e. protein components. Longer repetitions, with lower overload, are known as metabolic stimuli, and emphasize hypertrophy of the non-structural components of the muscle, such as glycogen and intramuscular water (sarcoplasmic components), and mitochondrial proliferation (Guedes Jr, 2003).

The target repetition ranges vary slightly, but generally comprise a:

Endurance: over 25-30 repetitions.

Muscular endurance: between 15-25 repetitions.

Hypertrophy: between 6-15 repetitions.

Strength: between 4-6 repetitions.

Maximum strength: 1-3 repetitions.

Intermediate or transitional repetition ranges are the intermediate counts between one physical capacity and another, which can develop both at the same time. For example, a high-intensity workout of 6 repetitions promotes improvements in both muscle hypertrophy and strength. A workout of 20 repetitions can promote improvements in the aspects of muscular hypertrophy and localized muscular endurance.

Some muscle groups are made up of a higher percentage of oxidative fibers (red fibers) than others, such as the abdominal muscles, calves and forearms. These seem to respond better to a high range of repetitions, so there is a tendency to use them more often than other muscles.

Training intensity: this is an extremely personal adaptation as it refers to the percentage of load for each repetition range used in each exercise. It is a parameter referring to the effort made by the student to overcome the resistance imposed on the muscles through the exercises.

Intensity is what will regulate the adaptation of the results obtained, since muscles can't count, they react to intensity, which is a biological adaptation, not a mathematical one.

All the repetition ranges have benefits in terms of performance and body composition, they just target the most obvious result.

Looking at the hypertrophy range, for example, which is around 8 to 12 repetitions, if a student is able to perform 3 sets of 8-12 repetitions with 100 kg on the bench press, but instead performs the same 3 sets with only 80 kg, they are not making the best use of their potential, because they have trained with only 80% of their maximum working capacity for this exercise. So it's not because he trained with 6, 8, 10 or 12 repetitions that he'll get that response. The intensity at which he uses these repetitions will determine his level of conditioning, post-training injury and subsequent muscle hypertrophy.

It may be that another student, doing the same 3 sets, but using 20 repetitions, but using 100% of their potential, gets a better response in terms of muscle hypertrophy. To emphasize: it's not the repetitions, but the intensity, which is the most important adaptation for regulating the gains a student wants to achieve.

Following the same line of reasoning, a student who trains at 100% intensity will obviously have an increase in pure strength, and this may be greater than that of another student who trains pure strength, but at an inadequate intensity.

In this respect, it should be borne in mind that it is not always appropriate or productive to apply 100% intensity in a training session, whatever the repetition range used and whatever the goal achieved. Students who don't periodize and always train at their limit expose themselves to the symptoms of overtraining and may suffer orthopaedic injuries. In addition, as the weeks go by, results will plateau and motor performance will even drop.

The correct periodization of training is very important, where periods of greater and lesser intensity are planned, enabling the athlete to continue training and obtaining results, preserving themselves from injury and boosting their results.

PART FOUR - TRAINING PERIODIZATION MODELS APPLIED TO BODYBUILDING

9. Training periodization: definition and context

The human body undergoes different processes of adaptation throughout life, mainly due to the environment in which it finds itself. For example, being in an environment with conditions that destabilize the body's balancing systems, i.e. conditions that disrupt the process of homeostasis, can have a direct influence.

Food, temperature, psychological aspects and physical training are some of the stressors that cause a breakdown in homeostasis. As a result of training, this breakdown of homeostasis generates fundamental benefits for the body, inducing it to rebalance itself, as well as increasing the body's resistance so that it can withstand disturbances of greater magnitude, resulting in overcompensation (Sequeiros et a., 2005; Minozzo et al., 2008).

However, simply generating successive overcompensations without proper evaluation, control and monitoring can lead to serious problems for the student, such as a plateau/drop in training performance and even health problems.

Therefore, we have to have an understanding of how to improve our students' physical abilities, as well as how to structure training programs correctly, respecting all the topics already presented.

Evaluating, monitoring and correcting a training program is hard work and, if done incorrectly, can lead to poor results. For this preparation and planning of training, the concept of Training Periodization is used, which is defined as a systematic, sequential and progressive approach to the planning and organization of training within a cyclical structure (Sequeiros et al., 2005).

In essence, this way of preparing the physical training program is designed to ensure adequate recovery between training sessions and to achieve optimum gains in the physical capacities of interest over an appropriate period of time.

Therefore, periodization is nothing more than a tool to facilitate the process of organizing a training program. Its applicability to bodybuilding is to control the training sessions in regular periods to promote the necessary break and this is where the big point lies.

It is important to note that in gyms, in general, the first stages of general preparation should be dedicated to the basic development of physical capacities, such as muscular endurance, aerobic capacity, strength and flexibility and exercise technique. And, of course, aesthetic goals will occur at this stage, but at the moment they are secondary goals in relation to the acquisition of a superior physical condition which, when achieved, allows the training to move on to more specific phases with greater safety, as well as further enhancing aesthetic goals.

Another positive aspect of periodized training is that it increases motivation by providing the necessary changes in variables over time and ensuring sufficient rest for adaptations to occur with greater emphasis. Also, planning at the start of training can motivate beginners, who generally tend to get discouraged at the start of training. This is linked to the fact that there is little variation in neuromotor learning, which can cause students to stop and return to training constantly.

In order to carry out such planning, it is necessary to know the development of the concept of training periodization throughout history and the existing models.

10. Linear periodization

Throughout history, the planning of training programs has been built on empiricism, with its first indications coming from Ancient Greece for the purpose of sports and military preparation. These concepts lasted for centuries, closely linked to the physical preparation of men during periods of war.

However, from the end of the 19th century and the beginning of the 20th century, European countries such as Germany and the Soviet Union began to use the concept of training periodization with greater emphasis.

In the 1960s, the first classic periodization model was proposed by Russian researcher Lev Pavlovich Matveev. This system was based on the theory of the General Adaptation Syndrome (Selye, 1959), which served as the basis for later training periodization models.

The classic periodization model proposed by Matveev can be summarized as a constant alternation between general training loads, which are related to physical capacities. Its main feature is to start the training program with high volume (more sets or repetitions) and low intensity (less weight) and gradually change the variables in order to reduce the volume and increase the intensity of the training sessions. These changes are made between 1 and 4 weeks.

Training progression model in a linear training periodization model.

Graph 2. Linear periodization graphically.

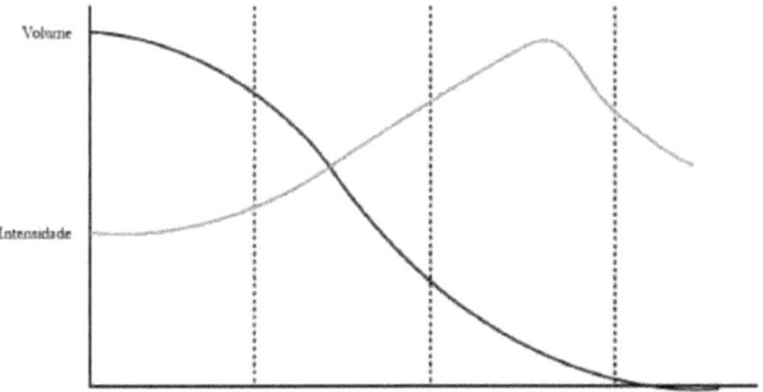

Adapted from Fleck and Simâo (2008).

This periodization model is defined in three phases:

Preparatory period: Three to four months (mainly in semester cycles) and up to five to seven months in annual cycles.

Competitive period: 1.5 to 2 months, which can extend to 4 or 5 months.

Transition period: From three to four weeks up to six weeks.

Figure 12. Periods in which the levels of organization are organized:

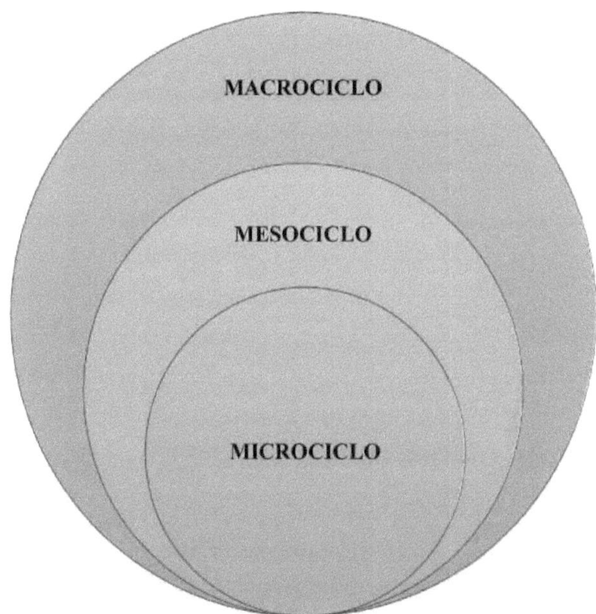

Macrocycle: involves a large part of the periodization, encompassing mesocycles and microcycles.

Mesocycle: represents the structure of the preparation, being a longer stage than a microcycle and usually lasting 2 to 6 weeks or microcycles (Bisquolo, 2010).

Microcycle: this is the smallest unit in the periodization process. It is characterized by training sessions and can be varied in periods according to the number of total sessions, usually totaling between 1 and 4 weeks of training, varying according to the capacity to be worked on.

Some findings in the scientific literature show the positive points of classic linear periodization, as in the study by Rhea et al. (2002) which demonstrated the development of maximum strength in healthy men who underwent 12 weeks of bodybuilding in linear periodization, and Prestes et al. (2006) found that bodybuilding training combined with aerobic training in a linear manner was effective in boosting the reduction of total fat and waist and abdominal circumferences.

Now, didactically, a good way to apply linear periodization is with beginners because it allows neural adaptations to occur in a more integrated way at this stage of training.

11. Reverse linear periodization

A variation of the classic linear training periodization model has been proposed and is called reverse periodization. As the name suggests, this model differs from the classic model in that it reverses the volume x intensity relationship, starting training with high intensity and low volume and over time decreasing the intensity and increasing the volume of training with a focus on promoting gains in muscular endurance (Rhea et al., 2003).

In reverse periodization, the initial phases of the program are characterized by low volume and high intensity, and as the training period increases, the volume increases and the intensity decreases.

There have been few studies verifying the effects of this type of training periodization. Rhea et al. (2003) compared different periodization protocols on muscular endurance and observed that, after 15 weeks of training, the group that underwent the reverse linear program developed more muscular endurance than the group that underwent the classic linear periodization. Another study by Prestes et al. (2009) compared the effects of 12 weeks of periodized training in women with 6 months or more experience and observed gains in maximum strength. However, there was no effect on body composition and strength development was lower than in the group that underwent classic periodization.

Didactically, because it starts training at a high intensity, this model doesn't seem to be the most suitable for beginners due to the adaptation to training mentioned above. In addition, it could be an interesting strategy for intermediate and advanced students as it offers variability in the training program.

12. Periodization in blocks

According to Gomes (2009) three phases characterize the evolution of training periodization models:

A: From its origins until the 1950s, when Matveev created the first classic training periodization model.

B: Between the 1950s and 1970s, training periodization models appeared that questioned Matveev's classic model.

C: From the 1970s to the present day, training periodization models have evolved greatly in terms of knowledge.

Despite this, according to Gomes (2009) contemporary models are based on four pillars for their systematization:

1: Individual training loads are justified by the body's individual capacity to adapt.

2: Concentration of training loads of the same orientation in short periods of time and the need to know in depth the effect produced by each type of workload and its distribution in the average training cycle.

3: Consecutive development of skills, using the residual effect of loads already worked.

4: Emphasis on specific training work. The necessary adaptations for high-performance practice with the implementation of special loads in practice.

The training periodization model proposed by Matveev was created on the basis of just one competition, which only allowed for one peak performance over the course of a season, which did not represent the real situation of the students. It therefore became necessary to create PT models that could provide multiple performance peaks over the course of the same season for different competitions such as national championships, world championships and Olympics. Two strands of thought emerged in response to this: scholars who were based on the PT model proposed by Matveev, and a second strand that completely disregarded this model.

Professor Yuri Verkhoshanki became one of the biggest critics of the training periodization model proposed by Matveev and ended up creating a totally different model to the classic one called Block Periodization.

Conceptualizing Periodization in Blocks

As the name implies, block periodization allows students to reach multiple peaks over the course of a season. For this to happen, the organization of training loads must be based on three concepts:

Programming: determining the strategy for structuring what is to be trained and the process by which the training will take place.

Organizational: practical implementation of the program, taking into account the real conditions and concrete possibilities of the athlete.

Control: criteria established in advance with the aim of periodically reporting on the athlete's level of adaptation.

Figura 13. Proposal for periodization in blocks:

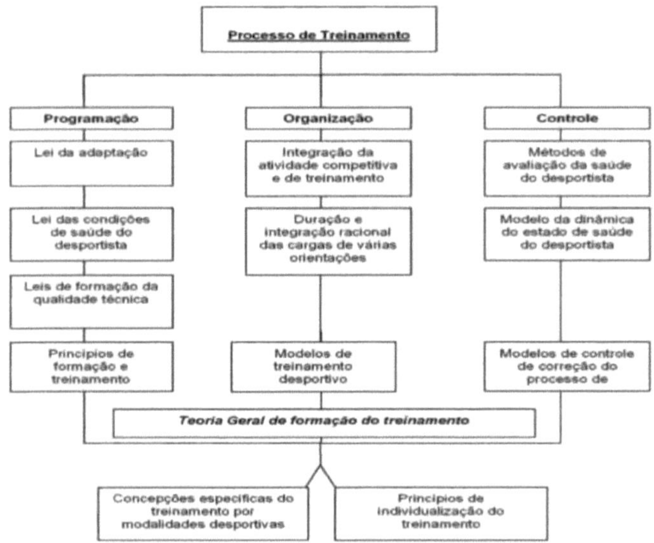

Taken from Gomes (2009).

As the name *implies*, training loads are divided into blocks. They are characterized by large amounts of load and are usually separated into three distinct blocks: **Block A:** Increasing locomotor potential (goal of special physical preparation).

Block B: Perfecting the skill of its effect in competitive exercise (objective of technical-tactical preparation).

Block C: High and secure competitive level (objectives of competitive and psychological preparation).

It should be pointed out that there is no obligation to have three specific blocks, since according to the energy requirements and specificities of each sport, the body's responses to the effects of training, the competition schedule and the specific goal you want to achieve, the training cycle doesn't necessarily have to contain all three blocks. However, block C will always be present in all cycles as it is the pre-competition block.

The block model is made up of a concentration of training loads aimed at improving strength in two or more training blocks every two and a half months, but despite the requirement for this main objective, the training loads are also aimed at developing other objectives in order to stimulate the necessary training effects. In addition, each block is not done in isolation, but as part of an overall training content with one block overlapping the next and so on, according to the principle of harnessing the effects of training.

For example, in block A, there is a large volume, the largest of the training phases, which should destabilize previously acquired performance levels, causing a physical, technical and tactical decrease due to fatigue and creating conditions for subsequent adaptations. It lasts approximately 12 weeks. In block B, the volume of training decreases to levels that allow the athlete's physical capacities to improve, preparing them for block C, where the main competitions are held. The graph below illustrates a periodization model in blocks:

Graph 3. Example of periodization in blocks.

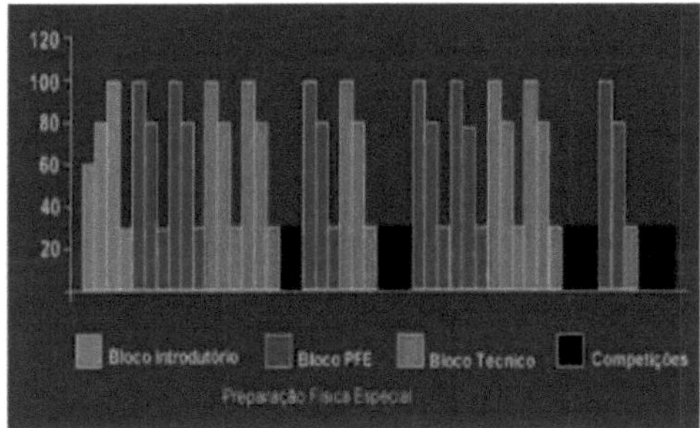

Adapted from Cometti (1991).

It's important to note that the block periodization model is based on the concept of the "Lasting Aftereffect of Training" in which the idea is that the effects obtained after successive training loads remain for a certain period of time after the end of training, i.e. training sessions in a concentrated block create conditioning bases for training the student's other abilities and improving technique. In other words, block training is based on the time during which the athlete still shows the effects of the previous training block.

Studies that have evaluated the effectiveness of block periodization have shown significant increases in the specific skills of their sports. It can be suggested that the concept of block periodization offers a reasonable approach for preparing students in sports that require a relatively small number of targeted motor skills, such as jumping. When preparing students who need to develop and excel in a larger number of specific sports skills, such as team, combat and endurance sports, block periodization does not offer the balanced multilateral training that allows students to achieve optimal athletic preparation and maximum performance.

13. Non-linear periodization

Non-linear or undulatory periodization is characterized by varying volume and intensity throughout the training period and is becoming increasingly popular among bodybuilders (Brown and Greenwood, 2005). It is the most recent of all training periodization models (Poliquin et al., 1988).

What makes this model different is that training intensities and volumes can be reduced and increased over short periods of time. What's more, variations in training loads can be made weekly, daily and even by muscle group during training sessions.

Some studies have shown that the high rate of frequency in the variation of stimuli has demonstrated the effectiveness of this training periodization model due to the stress imposed on the neuromuscular system, which is forced to adapt to different stimuli at all times (Rhea et al., 2002; Kraemer and Fleck, 2009).

This periodization model is a great alternative to break up the monotony of training, which contributes to better performance in training sessions. In addition, for advanced students, this model helps to maximize training sessions that use only one muscle group per day, making it possible to train quickly, intensely and with a wide range of stimuli.

14. Control of training loads

Initially, the paradigm of training periodization was done intuitively and the technical experience of teachers was fundamental for students to achieve their best results (Roschel, Trioli and Ugrinowistch, 2008).

Physical training is an organized and systematic process of improving physical capacities in their morphological and functional aspects (Roschel, Tricoli and Ugrinowistch, 2008).

Training periodization plays an important role in organizing all the variables involved in training. Controlling these variables allows you to control and monitor the load imposed by training.

Basically, training generates a "dose and response" relationship (Lambert and Borresen, 2010), so the improvement in performance or change in some physiological parameter (muscle hypertrophy, for example) resulting from a given dose of training as the physiological stress imposed on the body for a given training load.

Initially, loads were only controlled by the so-called "external training load". This represents the parameter of external variables linked to the form of training such as:

Number of repetitions

Number of series

Weight lifted

Interval between sets

Intervals between exercises

Number of exercises and order of exercises

Execution speed

And related to total work:

Force produced

Time on voltage

However, these variables do not represent the physiological and mechanical adaptations resulting from the training load.

Over time, sports scientists began to study how to boost results by analyzing and interpreting training performance over the course of the year and by analyzing the very little literature that had existed until then.

As a result, it has become necessary to quantify the training load, especially in terms of physiological parameters. This is what we call internal training load.

Initially, physiological variables were investigated using gold standard variables such as:

VO2: which is extremely useful because it is related to improved performance in various sports, especially cycling. However, its practical application is extremely difficult due to its lack of practicality, being limited to laboratory use. It is also unsuitable for intermittent activities such as weight training.

Lactate: is widely used to control and analyze training intensity, and is viable for intermittent activities. However, it is influenced by various adaptations such as diet, type of exercise and the individual's stress level.

So, despite its unquestionable validity, field practice is extremely difficult due to the different conditions, mainly representing the specificity of each sport. This is why indirect methods of evaluating the internal training load began to be considered. Among these, we can highlight questionnaires and self-reporting, but these have low reproducibility and validity in relation to gold standard variables (Shepard, 2003).

Other parameters that we can use to quantify the internal training load are: heart rate and subjective perception of effort, which are generally used in cycling activities and show good agreement. However, when we use these parameters in intermittent activities, we don't find this relationship. Despite this, subjective perception of effort is widely used in everyday life due to its extreme accessibility.

Borg (1982) defines the subjective perception of effort as the integration of peripheral (muscles and joints) and central (ventilation) signals which, interpreted by the sensory cortex, produce the general perception of performance during training sessions.

Recently, the subjective perception of effort has been investigated as a tool for monitoring the load of training sessions with greater emphasis. This model was proposed by Foster et al. (1996) with the aim of quantifying training load. The methodology is based on a questionnaire thirty minutes after the end of the training session regarding training intensity. Your answer is provided by questioning the scale shown below:

Figura 14. Borg scale adapted to quantify training session load.

Classification	Descriptor
0	**Rest**
1	**Very. Very easy**
2	**Easy**
3	**Moderaclo**
4	**A little difficult**
5	**Difficult**
6	-
7	**Very difficult**
8	-
9	-
10	**Maximo**

Taken from Foster et al. (2001).

In addition, Foster et al. (2001) give a score for the overall feeling of exertion. They also suggest an interval of 30 minutes so that light or intense activities carried out at the end of training sessions do not interfere with the results of the assessment.

But what's really interesting about this subjective perception of effort scale for quantifying internal training load is how it can be represented graphically, so that we can determine which sessions may be outside the expected training parameters. To do this, we need to use a unit of measurement called arbitrary units, which consist of calculating the score given by the athlete in relation to the total time of the training session.

Figura 15. Example of quantifying the load of training sessions.

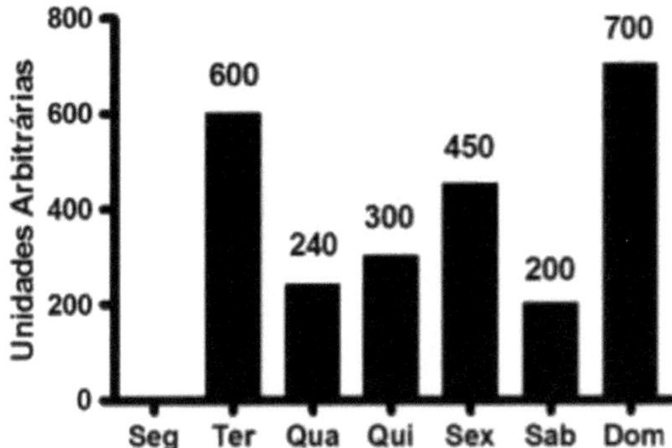

Taken from Foster et al., 2001.

In a nutshell, this graph shows the results of using the subjective perception of effort in a week of training in arbitrary units (which are the calculation of the intensity X volume of the training session).

Example of this calculation:

Friday: The training intensity was 9 X Session duration 50 minutes = 450 arbitrary units.

This graphical use is important because it is an excellent strategy for controlling training load in a simple and extremely effective way. For example, if we see monotony between sessions, this could suggest negative training adaptations, which could lead to the possibility of overtraining.

Despite being relatively new, it can be a low-cost strategy to use in our personal trainer classes and even in weight rooms (why not?). However, it's important to note that using perception requires caution, as you first need to understand how to assign scores for training sessions and then use them in your classes.

REFERENCES

American College of Sports Medicine. Progression models in resistance training for healthy adults. Med Sci Sports Exerc. 2009; 687-708.

Bacurau, R. F.; Navarro F. Hipertrofia, Hiperplasia: physiology, nutrition and training. Sâo Paulo: Ed. Phorte, 2001.

Badillo, J. J. G.; Gorostiaga, E. Fundamentos do treinamento de força: aplicação ao alto rendimento. 2. Ed. Porto Alegre: Artes Médicas, 2001.

Bàlsamo, S.; Simâo, R. *Strength Training for Osteoporosis, Fibromyalgia, Type 2 Diabetes, Rheumatoid Arthritis and Aging.* 2ª ed. Sâo Paulo: Phorte, 2005.

Barbanti, V. Aptidâo física: um convite à saù. Sâo Paulo: Phorte, 2003.

Basaldella, E. A.; Takeoka, A.; Sigrist, M.; Arber, S. Multisensory Signaling Shapes Vestibulo-Motor Circuit Specificity. Cell, 163 (2015), pp. 301-312.

Brown LE, Greenwood M. Periodization Essentials and innovations in resistance training protocols. Strength Cond J. 2005;27(4):80-5.

Enoka, R. Bases neuromecânicas da kinesiologia. 2. Ed. Sâo Paulo: Manole, 2000.

Faigenbaum AD, Kraemer WJ, Blimkie CJ, et al. Youth resistance training: updated position statement paper from the national strength and conditioning association. J Strength Cond Res. 2009; 23(5 Suppl):S60-79.

Fleck, S. J.; Kraemer, W. J. Fundamentals of strength training. 3.ed. Porto Alegre: Artmed, 2007.

Garber CE, Blissmer B, Deschenes MR, Franklin BA, Lamonte MJ, Lee I, Nieman DC, Swain DP. American College of Sports Medicine: Position stand. Quantity and Quality of Exercise for Developing and Maintaining Cardiorespiratory, Musculoskeletal, and Neuromotor Fitness in Apparently Healthy Adults: Guidance for Prescribing Exercise. *Med Sci Sports Exerc.* 43(7): 1334-59, 2011.

Guedes, J. D. P. Personal Training in Bodybuilding. 2ª Ed. Rio de Janeiro: NP, 1997.

Hopf, A. C. O.; Moura, J. A. R. Bodybuilding: the "detail" of terminology. Dynamics Magazine. V. 10, n.38, p. 18-23, 2002.

Kraemer WJ, Fleck SJ. Fundamentals of Strength Training São Paulo: Manole; 2009.

Mcardle, W. D. Exercise Physiology - Nutrition, Energy and Human Performance. 7ª ed. Rio de Janeiro: Guanabara Koogan; 2011.

Minozzo, F. C.; Lira, C. A. B. DE; Vancini, R. L.; Silva, A. A. B.; Fachina, R. J. DE F. G.; Guedes Jr, D. P.; Gomes, A. C.; Silva, A. C. DA. Periodization of strength training: a critical review. R. bras. Ci e Mov. 2008; 16(1): 89-97.

Moser AD de L, Malucelli MF, Bueno SN. Open and closed kinetic chain: a critical reflection. Fisioter Mov. 2010;23(4):641-50.

Okano, A. H., Cyrino, E. S., Nakamura, F. Y., Guariglia, D. A., Nascimento, M. A., Avelar, A., et al. (2008). Behavior of muscle strength and arm muscle area during 24 weeks of weight training. Revista Brasileira de Cineantropometria e Desempenho Humano, 10 (4), 379-385.

Poliquin C. Five steps to increase the effectiveness of your strength training program. Nat Strength Cond Assoc J. 1988;10(4):34-9.

Pontes, L.M.; Figueiredo Filho, A. Morphological and nutritional characteristics of juvenile students registered with the Paraibana Volleyball Federation. *Fitness and Performance Journal, v.9*, n.1, p.10-15, 2010.

Powers S.; Howley, E. Physiology of Exercise: Theory and Application to Conditioning and Performance. 5. ed. Barueri: Manole, 2004.

Prestes J, Frollini AB, Borin JP, Moura NA, Jûnior NN, Perez SEA. Effect of a 16-week program on the body composition of men and women. Rev Bras Atv Fis Saùde. 2006;11(1):19-28.

Prestes J, Frollini AB, De Lima C, Donatto F, Conte M. Comparison of linear and reverse linear periodization effects on maximal strength and body composition. J Strength Cond Res. 2009;23(1):266-74.

Prestes, J.; Foschini, J.; Marchetti, P.; Charro, M. A. Prescription and periodization of strength training in gyms. Barueri/Manole, 2010.

Rhea MR, Ball SB, Philips WT, Burketti LN. A comparison of linear and daily undulating periodization with equated volume and intensity for strength. J. Strength Com Res. 2002;16:25- 255.

Rhea MR, Ball SB, Philips WT, Burketti LN, Stone WJ, Ball SB, Alvar BA et al. A comparison of linear and daily undulating periodized programs with equated volume and intensity for local muscular endurance. J Strength Com Res. 2003;17(1):82-87.

Rocha, A. C.; Guedes Jr, D. P G. Physical assessment for personalized training, gyms and sports: a didactic, practical and current approach. Âo Paulo: Phorte, 2013.

Selye, H. (1959). *Stress,* the *tension of life.* Sâo Paulo: Ibrasa - Instituçâo Brasileira de Difusâo Cultural.

Sequeiros JL, Oliveira AL, Castanhede D, Dantas EH. Tudor Bompa study. Fitness & Performance Journal. 2005;4(6):341-7.

Simic L, Sarabon N, Markovic G. Does pre-exercise static stretching inhibit maximal muscular performance? A meta-analytical review. Scand J Med Sci Sports. 2013 Mar;23(2):131-48.

Terreri AP, Greve JMD, Amatuzzi MM. Isokinetic evaluation of the athlete's knee. Rev Bras Med Esporte 2001;7:170-4.

Teixeira, C. V. L. S.; Guedes Jr, D. P. Bodybuilding: Global body development. Sâo Paulo: Phorte, 2009.

Tubino, M. J. C. Metodologia cientifica do treinamento desportivo. 4 ed. Sâo Paulo: [s/e], 1985.

Vieira, F. G. Bodybuilding training methods: periodization and variations of the main training systems. 2. Ed. Sâo Paulo: icone, 2012.

Zatsiorsky, V. M. Ciência e pràtica do treinamento de força. Sâo Paulo: Phorte, 1999.

Printed by Books on Demand GmbH, Norderstedt / Germany